The Thriving Caregiver Journal

THIS JOURNAL BELONGS TO:

_____

PHONE: _____

EMAIL _____

Copyright © 2024

Designed by Carolyn Wheeler and
Joanna Andrick
Publisher: Meaningful Thoughts, LLC
ISBN: 978-0-9976764-9-5
Publication: 2024
Edition: 1
Printed in the USA

All rights reserved. No part of this book may be reproduced, distributed, or transmitted in any form or by any means without the prior written permission of the publisher, except for brief quotations used in reviews or critiques.

Daisy's Place™ The Thriving Caregiver™ Thriving Caregiver™ Caregivers helping caregivers™
The heart of our community.

For More Thriving Caregiver™ Resources Go To
ThrivingCaregiver.com

Welcome to The Thriving Caregiver Journal,

a place for your thoughts, prayers, questions, and quiet moments.

There's no structure here, no expectation, only space.

Whether you come to these pages to process grief, celebrate small wins, document your journey, or rest your heart in prayer, you are welcome just as you are.

Caregiving demands so much from you. This journal asks nothing. It's simply here to hold what you can't hold alone. Use it however you need. Return to it as often as you like. Let it become a companion on your journey.

These pages won't judge. They won't rush. They'll simply wait for you.

Love,

Carolyn

> "And let the peace of God rule in your hearts, to which also you were called in one body; and be thankful."
> Colossians 3:15 (NKJV)

Explore the full collection of books, journals, and planning tools at: www.ThrivingCaregiver.com

A portion of proceeds from this journal supports Daisy's Place, a nonprofit offering lodging, rest, and care for weary caregivers.
www.Daisys-Place.org

You're not alone, and you're always welcome here.

www.ingramcontent.com/pod-product-compliance
Lightning Source LLC
Chambersburg PA
CBHW052212090526
44584CB00019BA/3056